Isabel Losada

100

Reasons to be Glad

summersdale

100 REASONS TO BE GLAD

Summersdale Publishers Ltd
46 West Street
Chichester
West Sussex
PO19 1RP
UK

www.summersdale.com

Printed and bound in Singapore

ISBN: 1-84024-548-4
ISBN: 978-1-84024-548-6

PHOTO CREDITS

Babies can swim when their mums take them to proper baby swimming classes.

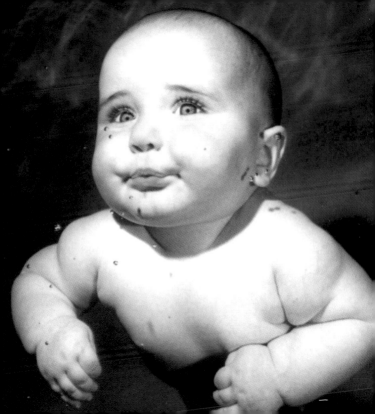

Spiders build **amazing webs** and sometimes **drops of rain** get caught and the sun lights up the picture.

The Dalai Lama teaches kindness and we can practise practising it.

That sometimes **a bus comes along** just as you walk up to the bus stop.

That **Bill Watterson** created Calvin and Hobbs. And if you've never seen these books you get to read them for the first time.

Cats choose to live with human beings.

It's really easy to **make pancakes.**

The **chance to smile** at strangers everyday.

The sea.

Wild poppies.

That **Rodin decided** to study sculpture.

That if you wake up really early you can **hear the birds** celebrating the arrival of the day.

A chance to **dance.**

Mandela. His life choices. And the fact he wrote *Long Walk to Freedom* so we can read about them.

The smell of **freshly cut grass**.

It only takes 30 days to **form a new habit**.

Unexpected new friends.

That **Morecambe and Wise**

met each other.

GANDHI

HIS TRIUMPH CHANGED THE WORLD FOREVER.

WINNER OF 8 ACADEMY AWARDS®
INCLUDING: 1982   BEST PICTURE

DVD
VIDEO

That **Richard Attenborough**
chose to make a film about Gandhi
and **kept going for ten years**
till it was made.

That sometimes people **forgive and forget.**

Old friends who say 'I admire you' or anyone who says lovely things that they don't need to.

The right to **education.** (Mandela had to wait five years in prison for the right to read a book.)

That **J. K. Rowling** didn't listen when she was told 'You'll never make any money writing children's books.'

Pushbikes. The best invention ever. Good free transport and fun too. Especially at night with lights.

Tantric sex.

Voluntary Service Overseas.

www.vso.org.uk

Giraffes.

Going for **long walks** is free.

That we live after the invention of **washing machines.**

That **trees have blossoms** in springtime.

That dentists can give you **injections** before they drill your teeth.

That the **moon looks the same** as it did the first time we saw it.

Rumi's passionate poetry.

It feels so lovely when someone says **'Sorry.'**

Thich Nhat Hanh and his writings on the practices of Buddhism.

Labrador **dogs chasing balls**.

That some people **enjoy cooking** and making food taste fantastic.

There are **monks and nuns** all around the world who pray for us every day and believe that 'in some sort of mystical way it makes a difference'. (Sister Helen OHP)

That **Juliet Stevenson** became an actress and Anthony Minghella wrote *Truly Madly Deeply* for her.

Chocolate.

The books of **Mark Salzman**. Especially *True Notebooks*, in which he teaches creative writing to juvenile offenders in a youth detention centre.

Currant buns.

That Robin Williams is in **so many** films.

Friends who phone when they are sad and lost and **ask you to support them.**

That they made advertising **smoking illegal** and for all those who lobbied to make this happen.

That **Barbara Hepworth**
became a sculptor.

Big Ben and the two peace protestors who climbed up to ask for peace because they cared enough.

That **John Nash** succeeded as an architect.

Listening to the radio is cheap.

The still small **voice of calm.**

That we have a **National Health Service** and every day doctors save lives.

School friends who you want to **stay in touch** with.

Old-fashioned **spinning tops** that hum.

That **Bach** wrote some cello suites.

That **Gene Kelly** was cast in *Singin' in the Rain*.

That we have **equal rights** for the disabled and more and more ramps for wheelchairs. (A long way to go but it's coming.)

Lambs. (And the fact that some people don't eat them.)

Snowfall.

That someone found out that the potato was edible.

New pillows.

Sandals.

That we can go to Speakers' Corner and **say whatever we want.**

Anybody who ever **loved** us – even a little.

A teacher helped us learn to read.

Tenderness.

Public libraries.

That our eyes can see colour.

Beach huts.

That we have **four seasons** and the weather is always changing so we all appreciate a sunny day.

Shark protection.

That Cole **Porter** and George **Gershwin** wrote songs.

Candles. The state of Peace. And any contribution that we can make.

That we can always give ourselves **another chance.**

That we live in a **multi-cultural** society.

The choice to **stay in** when it rains or the choice to **go out** and get wet.

All the **tunes** and all the lyrics in *My Fair Lady*.

The extraordinary work of **Dame Judi Dench.**

Fountain pens.

Anyone we know who can play a musical instrument.

Edinburgh.

We can all make the **world** a better place.

Trees – any trees – all trees – from any angle.

Our **favourite film** ever.

Puddles and the right to jump in them.

Breathing deeply makes you feel good.

The Internet. And the joy of e-mail that doesn't interrupt people's lives.

The first person we think of who **makes us laugh.**

Sea horses.

The smell of freshly **ground coffee** or your five most favourite smells.

WITZERLAND

PRISMALO 1 · SWISS MADE CARAN D'ACHE

Coloured pencils.

A glass of water.

That there is relative **peace** in Northern Ireland.

That **Mother Teresa** looked after the dying and her community is all over the world – especially in Baghdad.

Re-incarnation may be true.

We can always **do something different.**

Toast.

Digital cameras. I don't have one yet but maybe one day I will.

That we can send **birthday cards** to our friends.

That we can **swear** if we want to.

That you can **write** your own **list.**

www.summersdale.com